You Can Write

A

Million Dollar Memoir!

You Can Write

A

Million Dollar Memoir!

DAVID H. BURNS
(AKA, THE MEMOIR JUNKIE)

ISBN 978-1517198893

Acknowledgments

Thank you to all those who helped me along through life. Special thanks to the ones listed here:

Always to my Wonderful Wife Susie who also lives every day with the consequences of my memories, good and bad. A man could not be blessed with a better mate.

To others on my support team: Lisa, Jami, Aaron & Scott; always on my side.

More thanks to Susie for inspiration, encouragement and all the great tech help and editing work. I just love you to pieces!

Darlene and Bill, Bud and Donna too, thanks for the memories and the support along the road; as well as Les and Delores, gone but not forgotten for your saving me from the trash heap.

Della and Furman, Jim and Louise too. Various other Aunts and Uncles. And St. John's Orphanage in Fargo, North Dakota.

And thank you, Nat, for all the "techy" work.

God bless you each and everyone.

Contents

"Many people hear voices when no one is there. Some of them are called mad and are shut up in rooms where they stare at the walls all day. Others are called writers and they do pretty much the same thing."

—Meg Chittenden

CHAPTER ONE

Walk This Path
A Ways With Me

Welcome to the wonderful
world of memoirs, of writing.

This is a handbook to help you finally bring those long-simmering memories out into the open, crackling and sizzling to hungry readers everywhere. Thousands of people every year daydream about writing down some of their favorite, funniest or fiercest memories. Maybe you're one of them. It can be a daunting and bold task to tackle but also so very rewarding. Let's go down this path a ways together.

If you can write a simple letter and put in a bit of time studying the memoir genre, you can write a memoir. And if you can write a memoir, you can study a little more, rewrite and polish, and maybe write a popular memoir.

If you can write a popular memoir, with good timing and a great hook, you may be one of those who writes a Million Dollar Memoir! Especially if your story has a bit of drama and a good pinch of humor.

Am I going to say it's easy? Heck no. Are the odds against you? Oh yes. Is it really possible? Absolutely. It's been done so many times!

Do you have the necessary materials? Well, like I said above, if you have the basic skills to write a letter, and if you have average intellect, if you have even half a memory and lots of determination, you already have most of the tools necessary to reach for that golden ring of a Million Dollar Memoir!

And if you set your mind to it, if you do some serious study, at home or elsewhere, if you have a little luck, say a prayer and jump in with both feet, committed, the next Million Dollar Memoirist could be you.

The bad news is that you might burn out before you finish. Please, don't let that happen. Read some popular memoirs and do some memoir-specific study. Tell yourself you really can write a $1,000,000 Memoir!

Set a realistic time goal and plod along regularly toward it. The pages will stack up. A year might be realistic, (including careful rewrites). Maybe half that time if you're a real go-getter.

And set a monetary goal. A million, half a million, whatever is challenging to you. Something that will motivate you to strive for a sparkling manuscript.

But please, begin your memoir, work on your memoir, review and rewrite, and complete your memoir.

Some have second thoughts and ask, "Who would want to read about me, my memories?" Let me just say, as a self-proclaimed "Memoir Junkie," I love reading memoirs. Novels are fun too, and sometimes I pick up a how-to book or some other genre, but there's definitely something special about a good memoir. It's just such an enjoyable time to be allowed inside someone else's life for awhile, to discover what happened to them and how they responded. A true rendering. As I read, I wonder if I would have the courage to overcome many of the challenges they faced. To me it's a real privilege to walk awhile in a stranger's boots, to be allowed to experience just a bit of their environment, their real-life drama, their dreams, their failures, come-backs and victories. I am blessed by their generous spirit when they share a part of their life-story with me. My hat's off to memoirists for having the guts to allow us to peek in and walk a ways with them.

We can feel their elation when they've finally navigated through a really rough patch. We can feel their sadness during times of disappointment or loss. We laugh and even cry with them. We get to experience up close and personal a slice of the life of another human being and we are moved. We can often relate to their struggles and we grow fond of these brave authors. When a good memoirist reaches through the pages and touches us deeply we might even grow to love them. When that happens, you know you've found a one-in-a-thousand memoir. If it lingers on your mind long after you've finished reading it, if someone else's story causes you to change how you think about a topic close to you, if you want to reread certain sections or even the whole book, then you've found a one-in-a-million. And it just might be a Million Dollar Memoir!

Continue to study as you write. Barrington's "Writing the Memoir; from Truth to Art" is never far from my reach when I'm working in this genre. Last count I have about two dozen page corners dog-eared and perhaps portions of a hundred passages of her book highlighted. I refer to it often and I recommend that you have it or a similar instruction book handy to help you through a puzzling question and to encourage you to keep going. Another great guide for you is "Writing Your Life Story" by Bill Roorbach. Check it out, it's a winner.

Please don't blow off the advice to do a bit of study. If your goal is to write a worthwhile memoir or reach for that "Million Dollar Memoir," unless you're some kind of freaky genius, you must put in some serious time considering how the successful writers do it. Let's make your book worthy of you!

The good news is that many authors who have penned memoirs are not necessarily war heroes, famous politicians or athletes, hookers or Hollywood stars. Or even doctorate degree holders. Many are merely everyday types who happen to have a way of delivering their story that is immensely entertaining, they have what we call a wonderful "voice" on the page. And they have a real grabber of an opening, a really terrific "hook!"

Remember, you are the only person in the whole world who has the unique contents of your brain, your storehouse of memories. Relatives, co-workers and other people close to you all know parts of what your memory knows, but none have the entire ball of wax you do. Your memoir will be different from anyone else's, told from your own unique perspective, through the lens of your personal life experiences, education, the filters of your environment, emotions and your general slant on things: your very own written voice will come through. Let it come naturally, let it be you. You may have been told this before, but you're a one-of-a-kind person. Some good, some not so good, but certainly not exactly like any other person, and my friend, that's just how we, the readers of your upcoming memoir, want it.

One of the aspects of a Million Dollar Memoir is that it must be unique. And as stated above, you've got uniqueness in spades!

There are lots of ways to tell a story, and you might want to explore this; maybe you already have. Do you have favorite little incidents you've told and retold to friends or family members? Re-tellings that always receive enthusiastic responses? You were probably using good "voice" and maybe you could develop it for a book length memoir, if it's an authentic voice. Your re-telling must've been entertaining, and that's one of the main reasons people read, of course, is to be entertained. I believe we need more memoirs, we need to put our personal histories down on paper, or computer screen, or they'll be lost forever.

If you're more of a beginning writer it'll probably take you a bit longer to write your book and then rewrite it until it grows straight and tall like a rose stem right out of the ground, through the dirt and thorns, striving for the warmth and brightness of the sun, reaching its full potential and finally blooming into a beautiful, one-of-a-kind, bestselling memoir! Recognize your storehouse of memories as an amazing hidden treasure ready for the taking.

"But a Million Dollars?" you say.

"Yes," I say, "a Million Bucks!" (We'll discuss those delicious royalties a little later.)

Yes, just to reinforce what I mentioned above, I've set the goal high with my title of "You Can Write A Million Dollar Memoir" and I've done that for a couple reasons. I think it's a catchy title and titles help sell books (keep that in mind for when your own book is set to launch). I've also chosen that title because it's lofty, it's a challenge, it's a target worthy of the focus and the work you'll be doing to reach for it. Imagine if my title instead said "You Can Write A Ten Dollar Memoir." That just doesn't have the impact now does it?

I want this book, "You Can Write A Million Dollar Memoir," to be encouraging so when you doubt how realistic it is for you to reach for such a high goal (probably with trepidation), think about how many times it's been done already by others—many times. The memoir has been a hot-selling genre for a while now and continues to line the pockets of authors and publishers still today. You can realistically reach for a million dollar goal. If the memoir you write is entertaining, interesting, authentic, moving, amusing and you have the right publisher and a good chunk of old-fashioned luck, in today's vast market, you have a decent shot. It may not be at that level right off, when it's first published, but with word-of-mouth and marketing, maybe the continuing sales will reach your goals in the second, third or fifth years. Or it might just climb the bestseller list in the first few months!

But here's where most of us will come in; we may not hit that million dollar figure but maybe half of that, or even a quarter, and a quarter of a mill ain't so bad! What could you do with an extra $250,000 dollars that just whomped its way into your account from your own writing? How exciting to ponder! Or even just 100 G's for starters.

As I've said, it is important to set goals. If you're going to start a memoir, or any book, you should set a goal to finish it. Set a time goal so you'll keep working toward that time-line. You need to make this memoir of yours as good as possible too, something of which you can be proud. So you may want to set another, incremental goal to reach for, one to keep you reaching for the best memoir you can write. Like a monetary motivation. A million dollar goal is good. Of course, you can dial that back if you're more comfortable with a $500,000 figure or other mark. Set a goal to have your memoir published and to sell copies, lots of copies.

Although goals are important, the good news is that you don't have to set them all before you begin writing. You can start writing and see what might be a reasonable goal for yourself. You can also feel free to bend or reset your goals a bit later, but it's best to try to attain them if you can. I recommend you keep pushing ahead, perhaps 1000 words a day, two or maybe five pages day after day, a chapter a week or whatever. Some self-assigned quota to help you keep moving ahead. And after it's published, keep selling, pushing toward your monetary mark. How wonderful you will feel as each goal is conquered!

However if you're not looking to make a bundle on your memoir, that's fine too. Memoirs are written for many different reasons and it's a worthy goal just to complete one. Many parents and grandparents just want to put pieces of their past to paper for future generations. People who were raised up rough, like myself, or overcame addiction, and veterans all have stories to tell. Maybe you grew up with 7 or 8 siblings in a fun and lighthearted family. Or maybe you were a preacher's kid or a felon's. All can be fertile ground for a well-told memoir.

Storytelling is as old as the cave people and true

stories have always been popular. They're not going anywhere. And there are more readers coming along every year, more customers for authors, for memoirists!

Now, before we go any further, let's discuss what we're talking about here and what we're not. We're not talking about autobiographies. When I mention "memoir" I'm talking about the modern memoir familiar nowadays to most publishers, what they like to call a non-fiction piece of work, "a slice of life." Modern people often have short attention spans; they often do not have time or patience to read all about someone's entire life, every mundane detail. Choose a part of your life that has interesting consequences, just a slice within your whole life that can hang together as its own story.

You'll want to include other incidences that don't necessarily belong in this memoir, so if it feels awkward or out of place don't include it. Trust your gut. Here's the good part, hold on to pieces you cut, because you'll probably include those in your next memoir. Yes, with this "slice of life" approach you can write several memoirs each high-lighting a different aspect of your interesting life story.

CHAPTER TWO

Fun Study

"Becoming the reader is the essence of becoming a writer."

John O'Hara

Since you're deciding to be a memoirist you simply must read some modern memoirs. Don't look at this assignment as drudgery or some heavy homework assignment from your childhood. To me, this is the fun part. Memoirs get my juices flowing, get my mind flying along as I read about someone else's struggles, defeats and victories. I can't help but compare my own past at times, noticing the similarities and differences.

As you read, take note of how the author handles transitions moving from one time to another, changes in locations, and how certain events or happenings in the story affect your own emotions. Yes, literally take notes; you'll be glad you did. Notice the overreaching theme and focus of the story, threading its way through the pages. Sometimes it doesn't even seem to be present, like the author has lost it, but then there it is again, popping up in your face, showing you how the previous pages relate to the whole.

A perfect example of this is how Janette Walls, in her amazing memoir, "Glass Castle," shows her family trudging from one sparse shack to the next, one remote mining town after another. All the time, living through extreme poverty and family trials, her father works on the plans for his complicated gold-mining machine that will "one day soon" put them all on Easy Street and he'll be able to build his family an incredible castle made of glass! So well-rendered is this memoir that it sweeps you along through the seemingly endless tough times, with its magnificent hopes of relief just around the corner, and the dreamy promise of a spectacular castle made of glass. Of course, the castle, to the impoverished family, also represents full pantries, warmth, security and respect.

You will also need to develop a strong thread to weave through your slice-of-life memoir to hold it together. Walls shows us her struggling family trying to stick together, the forces against them and the glimmer of hope in the gold-mining machine and the sparkling glass castle helping to pull the story along. This "thread" I mention can be called the theme and you will need to have one for you own memoir. Think of it as an engine pulling the railroad cars on through the storms and battles, passing by the side-tracks. We can see these things as we pass by on the train, we can describe them and reflect on them, but we must be aware of the track we're running on and keep traveling ahead. When you reach the end of your book the caboose will be coming along behind, ready to wrap-up your story. The theme doesn't have to be well-defined in your head as you begin to write; it'll become evident soon with a bit of coaxing.

But we still have some planning to do before we get to that momentous ending. Even though we're writing non-fiction, still the story must have what writers call an "arc", beginning, middle and end. We have to open with a Bang!" We have to reach through the middle of the story for goals and plenty of barriers (stated or unstated), and then bring them all together in some kind of satisfying ending for the reader.

Your title, (and perhaps, subtitle), are very important in order to get readers interested enough to check out your book further. Of course, an attractive cover sparks initial interest too. The next important—extremely important—aspect of your book is the opening. You have to "hook" your prospect in order to make him/her a reader of your worthy story. The title may include a hook, and/or the opening scene may. If someone comes along and opens your book, you want to be sure there's action right at the beginning. It can be physical, mental or emotional but you want them to feel involved from the first page so they'll want to keep reading.

In the early draft of my memoir, "Kid On Fire," I opened with my family loading up a little truck in an Oregon logging town, getting ready to move half way across the country to Minnesota. But upon review with my professor at Writer's Digest University, we decided it would be better to open with something more dramatic, more of a "hook"! So I opened my memoir with a scene where my family has fallen apart somewhat and my brother, my father and I have returned to

Oregon and are living in a sparse little cabin. My mother has already died and my older sister has run away from Dad's violent ways. He comes home one night to the cabin, drunk, and shoots himself. Police flood the cabin and then try to pin the shooting on me or my brother, and my life is monumentally changed forever.

From there, my story unfolds in flashbacks and past details are filled in until the reader is brought up to the moment of the shooting. Then the engine of my story chugs further along the track, stacking up pages in the boxcars, toward its conclusion until the caboose comes into view through the smoke and dust as I wrap things up.

You just can't always begin at the beginning and expect the outcome you want. Start with a "Bang!" Pull that reader in the first moment!

As far as sharing your written work with trusted readers along the way, before it goes to the publisher, you simply must! You need to run it past trusted readers who'll give you honest feedback. As clever as you are, you can never be as objective about your own work as someone else can be. Your trusted readers will spot little things you may have overlooked, and maybe some larger themes or contradictions. You certainly don't have to take every or any suggestion that's offered but it's wise to carefully consider and appreciate a reader's input. Don't get defensive; they're most likely on your side.

Once you've completed the rewrites, made the necessary changes and worked out the kinks, then it's time to run it past someone else again prior to publishing. If they're sharp, they will always find more needling little mistakes or places of confusion. You want to get your memoir as free of mistakes as possible.

Remember, if an intelligent stranger can't make sense of a paragraph or sentence, or they have to guess at what you mean, you do not have clarity. And if a piece of writing needs anything, it needs clarity to succeed!

Keep reading successful memoirs as you plan your own. Study them and take more notes. You can learn so much that will help you along with your own work.

Frank McCourt, in his award-winning memoir, "Angela's Ashes," writes with the authority of a young Irish/Catholic lad growing up in extreme poverty in Limerick, Ireland. Even though his Irish background and heritage aren't everyday familiar to most people in the world, they color his writing beautifully. His voice on the page, (and later, screen), is rich; it sings and dances before your eyes. It's as if he's right there with you telling you his story, no frills, no false sophistication. Just your Irish pal Frank telling you how it was.

Another good example of voice on the page is the memoir by Mary Karr, "The Liar's Club." A small whip-stitch of a girl growing up in rough Texas oil towns talking to you about how things were, how she remembers it all.

Check out some successful memoirs.

CHAPTER THREE

More About Voice

"We are a species that wants to be understood who we are. Sheep lice do not seem to share this longing, which is one reason why they write so little."

ANNE LAMOTT

How is your voice on the page going to come through? Will it be low-key and ponderous? Maybe not so good. Will it be full of tongue-in-cheek humor? Oh, what fun! Will it be artificial and full of over-the-top claims? We certainly hope not.

Have you ever been button-holed at a party by a braggart? Someone you knew from the moment he opened his mouth was used to extreme exaggeration beyond belief? Well, if he wrote a memoir and you began reading it, what would you think? You'd know it was not truth and you probably wouldn't appreciate his silly attempts to convince you it was. Respect your readers, they're a clever bunch and can smell a rat pretty quickly.

Your voice must be a product of you, your background, your environment, your family, your education, your own experiences, your faith and outlook on life, and your own mind-set. And so many other aspects that makes you specifically who you are. Be as truthful as you can, be interesting and colorful or humorous; but above all, be you on the page. How do you speak? How do you turn a phrase? What kinds of phrases do you often use? Do you speak in long, complicated sentences or are you more of a clipped, short-response sort? Put it on the page.

Let your story flow. Don't stop to correct spelling and reflect too much initially about previous pages. Leave that for later, right now you're chugging down that train track, stacking pages in the boxcars. When you see how far you've come with your project, you'll be encouraged to repeat that the next day, or exceed that mark.

Go back the next morning, or next time you sit to write, and read over the past day's pages. Remember, a complete stranger will have to decipher your voice-on-the-page and make sense of it. If it's too accented, too full of jargon, too foreign in any way to grasp, you may be in trouble and have to tone it down. A reader will not have your speaking inflections or gestures to make your meaning understandable. Your voice must be you but also clear or you'll lose your readers.

Spend some time becoming comfortable with your written voice. Once you start your book we don't want it to vary much. You wouldn't want your thick beef gravy to suddenly reveal sour shards of dill pickle, for instance. Be consistent with your voice. Just like those chunks of pickle in your gravy, an inconsistency in your written work, something with a completely different voice, (or flavor and texture), can jar the reader (or eater) in an unpleasant way. A bad taste in the mouth can result in a bad review or cause the reader to throw the book away mostly unread.

A Montana country boy won't just begin to tell his story with the voice or perspective of a kid from Brooklyn, New York. It's just not natural or believable.

Let us hear your voice on the page, let us discover who you are. I'm sure you will be warmly received in the Great Brotherhood & Sisterhood of Memoirists on your own merits! Naturally narrate your life's story.

Take a look at Sudie Gal's very direct voice in this example from her memoir, "DOLLARS TO DONUTS: A Family's Strain of Insanity, My Stormy Walk of Faith Through It, And That Whole Crazy Mother-Daughter Thing." Sudi Gal gives you the feeling that she is a woman you would enjoy meeting and having as a personal friend. A woman of deep spiritual belief and a person of strong ethics. And although she's been deeply wounded in her struggle with a demented and ruthless mother, she's finally come to deal with it, as well as one can, without assigning blame to her mother or herself for the tragic ending of their relationship. Sudie Gal's voice reveals so much to us in this short piece from her book. Buy a copy as soon as you can and read it slowly, study how the story rolls along naturally from a devastating flood, to more complications than the reader can imagine, and on toward the complete dissolution of a once-close family. Feel your heart break, along with this talented author's, as she pours out her memoir...

I learned as a child to always strive to do the right thing and to do everything as best you can or don't do it at all. As I've aged and matured as a follower of Jesus, I've realized just what that really looks like. It looks like forgiveness when it comes to healing one's own hurts. Your own forgiveness of others and of yourself... your earnestly seeking forgiveness from others and from God. And claiming the blessing of that forgiveness as your own healing begins from there.

As you read and study this example, pause a moment and look inward. Just as Sudie Gal reached such a gracious point in her life, in reflection of those tumultuous years with her aging mother, in the end she was so forgiving. I hope in your own memoir you can reach a similar point with those who people your story. I urge you to stay away from old feelings of revenge and harbored ill will. I strongly believe that you will be happier with your finished manuscript if you do.

CHAPTER FOUR

Color Inside The Lines

"But I see your true colors, Shining through;
I see your true colors, And that's why I love you."

WRITTEN BY BILLY STEINBERG
AND TOM KELLY; SUNG BY CYNDI LAUPER

While we want to write a unique memoir, we want to be sure to keep within the guidelines of our genre if we're going to call it a "memoir." Memoir is one of several genres within the category of Non-Fiction, so your memoir is a non-fiction piece. It is factual. Please keep this in mind. If you're going to write fiction, write fiction. You can choose to write fiction based on fact, or based on a real-life story, but you must be up front with the reader what your story is. If you're going to write memoir, you're writing non-fiction.

There are certain freedoms you have when you write, certain places where you can carefully bend the rules a bit. But not where it's going to substantially change the story, or wrongfully show someone in a poor light. If you stretch the truth too far, you can wind up in court, so be careful. Or if you wander too far from fact, you may certainly come across to the reader as inauthentic. If that happens, your book will probably end up in the trash can. Also, if you're not as honest as you can be, you could really harm relationships. There's always someone out there in the reading audience to call you on fabrications.

One place it's generally acceptable to color outside the lines a bit is when you reconstruct dialogue. Nobody remembers very many conversations word for word. However, you may remember bits of a long ago conversation, the gist of it, kind of how it went. Someone smarter than me, said even if you can't remember what exactly was said, "your skin remembers." To me, that means that even though your memory can't come up with the words that were exchanged, you subconsciously know the essence of what was said, your emotional memory captured the conversation on some level. You know how the conversation made you feel, the mood of it. That's probably enough for you to recapture that conversation as honestly as you can, the basic truths of what was said. Famous memoirist, Bill Roorbach, in his indispensable "how to" book, "Writing Life Stories," tells us to do our best ethical reconstruction of the conversation. "And if I'm really going out on a memory limb, I'll say so: admit to making plausible dialogue, then carry on," he tells us.

In the next paragraph Roorbach reminds us that although truth and honesty are immeasurably important in memoirs, drama is even more so, if you want to have a successful book. He says, "Drama, characters in action, must be the first excellence. Accuracy comes in a very close (and very important) second but second." I might put *clarity* on that priority list as well, maybe even right on top: Clarity, Drama and Accuracy. You must have clarity to have a decent written piece. Don't make readers guess at your meaning.

Another place you have a certain artistic license to carefully bend the rules in memoir writing is with the time frame of your story. You're allowed to telescope time instead of trying to tell every event that took place that year, or week, or day. You can condense time in your memoir if it does not substantially change the truth. By "telescoping," I mean that you can cheat with your time frames a bit if the outcome doesn't alter the story noticeably. For instance, in my own case I've lived in 30 some locations, some for very short periods, so I feel free to lump two or three scenes in one little logging town when in fact a couple of the scenes actually took place elsewhere. It's not paramount to the story that my father smashed up his black Buick in Canyonville, Azalea or near Devil's Flat, all places we lived in Oregon. The story's basically the same if we were living in one little logging town or another. Lumping a few months together, and where we lived, saves me from describing each temporary location. I do note to the readers that we moved around a lot during this time period to give them a more accurate feel for our lifestyle.

You must skip times that do not apply to the story you're telling or that do not advance the story arc. You can also switch things around a bit to reshape the story if it keeps the basic truth intact but illuminates the overall story better for the reader.

Always keep in mind the word "carefully" when you stray from the exact facts. Cut, reshape, and telescope to improve the story, but do so carefully and with the best, honest gut you can. Never try to falsely reshape the story to get even with someone in your story or to show them in a less-than-honest light. Every person has good and bad characteristics. Portray the players in your book evenhandedly, everyone deserves that. Lots of people are going to read your book, be a respected and honest author.

If you want to protect someone's identity, you can change the name if you wish. In my memoir "Kid On Fire" I changed the name of a neighbor boy that was such an evil teen I felt compelled to hide his identity. I've heard over the years that he has become a pretty good member of society (even though, among other things, he had a propensity to torture animals when I lived down the road from him long ago and I don't really trust that he could change very much at the core.) I even took it a step further in my memoir when I combined his character with another boy who had questionable scruples as well. I did it to expedite things.

If you choose to use some of these artistic techniques, it works well to let the reader know upfront what you're doing. Right up front near the title page a simple statement will usually do. "For pacing and clarification at times the author has taken liberties with aspects of time passage. Certain names have been changed to protect the identity of characters in the story. Dialogue has been reconstructed as closely as memory allows." This should keep you free of guilt and your tail-end out of a sling. So try hard to stick to the truth but keep that story flowing!

Do not let lack of absolute accuracy freeze you up. Deal with it, be honest with the reader, and move on. Remember, you're a memoirist not a journalist.

CHAPTER FIVE

What Experts Mean By
"Show Don't Tell"

"Memory resides in specific sensory details."
JUDITH BARRINGTON

You must find some interesting scenes to show to your readers. As any writing instruction book, manual, blog, article or teacher will tell you, or perhaps has told you, "show don't tell."

As you're bouncing along happily recording how your slice-of-life unfolded, you must watch for those interesting places where merely telling simply will not do. Telling works for awhile, i.e., "We moved to the coast that year, the North Oregon Coast." Then this happened, then that, and so on. Telling can really cover some ground but slow down to show.

Watch this example of "show don't tell" from some of my own work.

That year my older brother, Buddy, and I bought a car together. Buddy cleaned the spark plugs, I fixed up the rusty exhaust system, and we sold it for a profit.

Okay, something like that may be fine in your memoir. It hints at a pretty good relationship between the brothers, reveals that they know something about cars, and they're working to get ahead.

~~But now let's flesh it out a bit and *show* them working to get ahead~~.

Guess I was about 14 or so, and Buddy was 16 when he found a 1946 maroon, Nash for sale cheap. He came in, his hazel eyes twinkling, to tell me about it.

"Let's buy this thing, fix it up and sell it," he said, sucking me right in. He pulled $32.50 out of his jeans pocket and slapped it on the table. "Match it, and we'll split the profits." Buddy knew that's just about what I had saved up after a summer of strawberry picking at a valley farm and I couldn't get my money out fast enough.

It was just a nine-year old car and pretty straight. The gravel-pitted front end and sun-faded paint on top revealed some age, but there were no broken windows and hardly any body damage. Buddy started it up with lots of grinding and pumping on the gas pedal and it sputtered and smoked, but started.

Once we got it home Buddy went to work on the spark plugs. He disconnected the wires, unscrewed and removed the plugs. He scraped and cleaned the contacts and carefully reset the gaps for full spark potential. With a small piece of sandpaper he brought the points to a fine shine then replaced the plugs. And he adjusted the gas flow to the carburetor.

Meanwhile I was underneath on my back in the gravel working on the exhaust system. I'd found a couple Hills Brothers Coffee cans at the dump (our go-to supply house), I split them up the side and wrapped them around the loose tail pipe joints. Then I clamped them around the pipes as tight as I could with stiff clothes hanger wire (stolen from our foster mom). I jimmied up the whole rattly assembly to the frame under the car as high as I could get it, avoiding any direct contact with the gas tank, (didn't want any unexpected explosions) and called it good.

We took it for a test run afterward and it was running pretty smoothly and the previously blaring exhaust was down to a mild roar. I remember the radio in the maroon and wood-grain dashboard of that Nash like it was yesterday. It lit up from within like a small jukebox of the day and had a row of square buttons you could push to change the previously-set stations. The trouble was, we were so far from any town in the Oregon Coast Range, the only station that would crackle to life was KTIL in Tillamook 30 miles toward the coast, but that didn't stop me from playing with the buttons as I repeatedly searched for another station. Mostly I had loud static but didn't give up until Buddy said, "Knock it off! I'm trying to drive here!"

Buddy sold the Nash for $125 about a week later and we bought school clothes with the profits. I was sad to see the new owner drive that car away, mildly roaring toward town and better radio reception.

You can see how much more information is imparted in this example than the previous "telling" version by making it into a scene. By showing rather than telling we draw the reader into the action.

Your scene doesn't have to be earth-shattering, deeply dramatic or knee-slapping funny. Once you get the readers on-board they're along for the ride and they may even find some day-to-day activities interesting. In the example above, hopefully, readers are curious about how a couple young teenage brothers in the 1950's pull together to survive. Readers are probably rooting for the brothers to succeed too, and that's always a good thing.

Explore your own work to find places where you can take a section from bland "telling," to more interesting "showing." It's fun to relive some of those moments, to reconstruct them as best you can, and it's more entertaining for the reader. Build your scenes step by step, word by word; you can do it!

CHAPTER SIX

Verbs

(The Live Action Heroes
of Every Sentence!)

*"I have forced myself to begin writing when I've been utterly
exhausted, when I've felt my soul as thin as a playing card...
and somehow the activity of writing changes everything."*

JOYCE CAROL OATES

Picture Dr. Frankenstein's famous laboratory. Dr. F.
is slumped over on a stool looking whipped,
beaten, depressed. Why? Because for weeks, months
and perhaps even decades he has dreamed of, worked
day and night, stolen body parts in his attempt to build
a patched-together human-like monster that he brings
to life. He constructed a complicated high-voltage-
spark-of-life machine and done who-knows-what-
beyond belief to stitch together his monster. Then he

hooked his creation up to the gigantic power source and flipped the switch! Bright flashes of light sizzled all over his laboratory and his frightened little humpback helper, Humpy, dove under a table! Lights all over the village dimmed and twittered. But the monster showed no signs of life. Dr. F. tried again and again switching the power on. To no avail. Sadly the monster had no verve, no verbs. No life. The end.

That's kind of like a story that ran out of verbs. In the end it doesn't go anywhere. It's disappointing. It's really no story at all without life. The monster did not jump (verb) to life. It didn't breathe (verb), or walk (verb) or move (verb) or see (verb). It didn't feel (verb) or moan (verb) or chase (verb) anyone, or slurp (verb) coffee. It had no verbs. And without verbs it just laid there, a morbid and sad horizontal scarecrow. A scary monster needs life to be scary, or at least interesting. It needs to do something. It needs action verbs.

Writers need verbs too, preferably strong verbs. A story needs life! Action! Electricity to spark some kind of action! It needs verbs, the Live Action Heroes of any sentence! Pack your writing arsenal with rich verbs and you'll go a long way.

As you go back over your work constantly check for lazy verbs and try to change them out for fresher, livelier ones.

Example from my own arsenal:

My wife recently adopted a tuxedo kitten, black and white and full of zip. She named him Skeeter. We have come to find out Skeeter loves to grab ball-point pens whenever one's within his reach; he just loves a good pen. (We think he may be a writer some day.) He likes to bat them around on our bare wood floors.

The other day I was sitting there in my lounger

when out of nowhere here comes Skeeter whipping across the living room floor sliding a pen along with him. We have two grown daughters about 170 miles away and I like to keep them abreast of our current affairs. I thought about writing them that "cute little Skeeter zipped through the living room sliding along a pen as he went." While typing the email, I thought the verb "batting" was maybe not quite what I wanted. What was Skeeter's action like? What did it remind me of? Ah! After a moment it came to me and I wrote:

Dear Girls, Skeeter has been great fun, always up to something to make us laugh. A little bit ago he hockeyed a ballpoint pen through the living room at high speed and down the hall toward some unseen goal...

Isn't "hockeyed" fresher and more fun than "sliding along?" I think so, and it certainly gives one the image of a hockey player zigzagging across the flat ice with a puck. Very much like Skeeter with the pen across the wood floor. And he didn't even need a hockey stick. Always look for fresh verbs.

Also be on the lookout for weak verbs. Strong verbs breathe life into mundane sentences. Here's another example from my own work:

I wanted that Schwinn Bicycle in the store window so bad!
Or is this better?

I'd plant myself outside the store window studying the Schwinn bicycle until my feet fairly ached to be on those shiny black foot pedals—just a blur, with my hands clamped around the handlebar grips as I'd pump up the steep hill on Foster Street toward home.

"Hill? What hill?" I'd yell as I crested the hilltop astride the Schwinn in my mind!

29

The one verb in the first example above is "wanted." Not very active.

Verbs in the second example include: *plant, studying, ached, clamped, pump, yell,* and *crested.* Seven hard-working verbs that draw the reader into the scene! That's what we want.

Just to reiterate, if you're in the flow of a sentence, you don't need to stop right then to find a great verb, you may want to keep the flow going. Later, during rewrite, you can send out a search party and capture just the sparkling verb you need. And, yes, you will need to rewrite. Maybe multiple times; you want this material to be something you'll be proud of. Some say rewriting is what begins to separate an amateur writer from a pro. You certainly want to strive for pro-hood if you're reaching for a Million Dollar Memoir!

CHAPTER SEVEN

Limits of Memoir

"I think of an author as somebody who goes into the market-place and puts down his rug and says, 'I will tell you a story' and then he passes the hat."

ROBERTSON DAVIES

L et's consider Ivan Doig's memoir, "Heart Earth," a tribute to his late mother. Doig, if you don't know, is a wonderful, award-winning author of more than half a dozen books, all well worth your time. Notice how the words in the title are practically the same word, just shift that "H" from one end to the other. And if you think about it, the title just about shouts the love Doig's mother had for the rugged Montana ranch land they lived in, "my heart is in this earth."

Most memoirs are written in first person by the person who lived that slice-of-life, those scenes, personally. However, there are techniques an author can use to record happenings that took place when he or she was not a direct eyewitness. In "Heart Earth" Doig relies heavily on a packet of letters between his mother in Montana and her brother on a Pacific battleship during World War II. Doig himself was a youngster of five and six at the time and recalls moments here and there, and reading the letters decades later helped fill in a lot of details not noticed or understood by the youngster at the time.

In one long scene while his mother, Burneta, is in the high country herding sheep alone, in spite of his absence and no description of this day in the letters, Doig imagines the details. He lets the reader know right away the technique he's employing, and carries it off beautifully. This is not a common way to write a section of a memoir and for it to work it must be executed very carefully. Watch how Doig pulled it off.

"Sixteen kinds of weather a day this year," I can imagine Burneta saying to herself as she unties the yellow slicker from behind the saddle and slips it on. Knots the saddle strings firmly down on the mackinaw jacket she'd been wearing since she left the cabin and climbs back on Duffy to ride through the sun shower...

And on he writes for several pages basing it all on imagination. "But it's memoir," you scream, "how can he do that? He wasn't even present to see what Burneta was doing." But it rings true, and Doig pulls it off because the reader knows as a young boy he has seen his mother rounding up sheep time and again. He has an authentic voice.

If you try such a technique, be up front with the reader, let them know what you're doing, i.e., "I wasn't there myself but here's how I see this...".

Now, in another example, watch how I handle a similar dilemma in showing a scene in my memoir, "Kid On Fire," ~~when I wasn't an actual witne~~ss, or maybe just too shocked to remember seeing it. I was about seven when this took place in our rented trailer.

It might've been while we lived in Willmar, Minnesota or before, that Dad got so mad at one of Mama's acquaintances. Let's call him Charlie. ~~I don't recall actually seeing it all happen,~~ but from what I've been told is that it went down something like this: Dad had been gone awhile and Mama was entertaining Charlie. Dad must've known it was Charlie's car parked out front when he got back, and he strode inside and apparently directly to the knife drawer.

Right away there was loud talking and scuffling sounds from inside the trailer. Then, I'm told, the door flew open and Dad had a butcher knife at Charlie's throat, holding him from behind. There was some struggling, pushing and shuffling of feet as they slowly stepped out of the trailer onto the ground, Dad's knife holding steady at Charlie's throat. Mama seemed to have hold of them both from behind and pleaded and begged as they moved like one unit toward Charlie's car.

"Jim, don't do it! Don't do it! Let him go!" Mama said.

Dad pushed Charlie hard, right smack into the side of his car as he dragged the knife sharply against Charlie's throat.

"Get outta here, you son-of-a-bitch! And stay away!"

Mama screamed and Charlie made a confused sound, "Uhhh?" He managed to stay on his feet and grabbed for the door handle as he checked the wound at his throat with the other hand. The blood had come right away and covered his hand as he looked in horror. Mama dashed back into the trailer and came back with a towel for Charlie as he settled into the driver's seat. He took the towel and held it to his throat as he started the car.

"Git outta here, you bastard!" Dad yelled as Charlie pulled

away towards the road in a cloud of dust. And we thought that'd be the last we saw of Charlie around there, but we were wrong. When Dad was gone Charlie would still show up to see Mama, even with his neck all bandaged up. Some folks like to live dangerously, or they're just painfully slow learners.

With his reputation, I don't know why anyone would want to test Dad's temper. I sure wouldn't. He told me one time that even though we weren't very big (he was tall but quite thin), "Don't be afraid to pick up an equalizer." By that, of course, he meant a knife or a gun, a rock or a wrench. I never saw Dad look inside a Bible but I'm sure he was familiar with the story of David and Goliath where much smaller David used a rock to bring the monster down!

Notice that I'm honest with the reader and admit that I don't actually recall witnessing this scene, but relying on the accounts I'd heard about it. I'm really not sure today if my little seven-year-old-self saw it happen or not. A counselor explained to me once that when a young kid is witnessing too much violence in one stretch, sometimes safety modes in his brain can stuff some of it into deep black holes. It's a specific type of amnesia called dissociative amnesia where the brain blocks overwhelming memories for a time period. But it's fair game to include this scene in my memoir because the story was told to me and the re-telling is in my memory banks. The story certainly says a lot about how I grew up and was affected by another one of my parents' violent actions. I've imagined some details for story's sake and continuity. Readers want to believe the story is an honest one, but remember they demand a good story. To succeed you must figure out how to deliver both.

The example above is basically what happened, however our family was moving around so much there for a couple years, I'm not sure if it actually happened before we left Oregon, in Minnesota or North Dakota. But trust me, it did happen, and that's what I wanted to show the readers. It's not all that important exactly where it took place. This is the sort of thing I'm talking about when I say, "Show your scene with an honest gut." Not every detail can be shown exactly as it occurred, but the story is an honest one.

Memoirists, of course, can be nervous about putting relatives in their stories, revealing family skeletons and secrets. Siblings may object to your telling about certain things done or said by parents or themselves years ago. Sometimes the author shows parts of their story to living relatives before publication for approval. I do not recommend this. It could open up big controversies and completely kill your memoir before it even gets off the ground. For you to be a successful memoirist you must have a certain boldness, even if it's not a trait of your usual character.

Please don't misunderstand me. You can be reasonable in your rendering. Don't set out to hurt someone, do not be cruel, but have enough grit to tell the truth. Anne Lamott, in her amazing book, "Bird By Bird," said, (I'm paraphrasing), if they didn't want to be written about, they should've behaved better.

You're the author of this piece, not them. At times we authors have to walk a very fine line. Complainers can try their hand at their own memoir if they think it's so easy. But remember, this is your story to tell.

At some point you have to come to grips with hard choices. I found it difficult for many years to write anything that sounded judgmental, especially toward my parents. Although my early home life was anything but Christian, the Biblical message to "honor thy mother and thy father" jumped up in my face. But the more I read honest, popular and Million Dollar Memoirs, or opinions about how to write them, the more I realized I just needed to present the honest truth as well as I could and let the reader come to his or her own conclusions. God will judge; He knows the whole story already.

Once I began to release myself from keeping the nasty little and large family secrets, the more weight I felt off my shoulders and the easier the blood seemed to flow through my heart. There's a good Tom Hanks movie called "The Road To Perdition" where he portrays a likable gangster. He's involved in all kinds of illegal situations but has this deep love and protective umbrella over his young teenage son. (Spoiler alert): When the mob turns against Tom's character he shoots his way out of trouble, killing several previous associates, only to be shot in the back and killed by a coward a short time later.

Flash forward a bit, the boy is telling some of the story and the listener asks, "Do you love your father?"

Without hesitation the boy replies, "He's my father."

That's about where I've finally come to rest at when I think about my own father. He had his good points. He was an amazing mechanic, he would go to battle for innocent animals, he loved flowers and he was gentle with Mom and us kids most of the time. Of course I've been conflicted about him all my life, but I am doing my best to be forgiving. I know he had an extremely tough childhood as well, and I try to be persistent in my forgiveness.

You may have to work out similar things in your own mind and heart about family members or friends.

When I was very young I remember my father beating my mother, slapping, shaking, choking and sometimes worse. Sometimes he beat us kids too. He could be a very violent man. My mother was no angel, I've learned with age, but there's so, so much I'll never understand. I just know my father could be so rough, so scary. They both drank heavily but there's no excuse for such beastly behavior.

As I show in my memoir, "Kid On Fire," my young, still-forming emotional make-up suffered deeply from my violent start in life. My older sister and brother seemingly fared a bit better. At some point I came to believe I must write about my young life, threw caution to the wind and plunged in. My folks should have behaved better. But, in spite of it all, like the boy in the movie, I love my parents. Maybe they did the best they could with the cards they were dealt in life. If, someday, I see them in Heaven, I hope they understand why I've handled things the way I have. I feel I'm doing the best I can with the cards I've been dealt. Admittedly, there are some terrible memories I withhold from my memoir because I just don't think they'll improve my book. Just because you've decided to become a memoirist, as I have, it doesn't mean you have to bite off every wart or squeeze every pimple in public.

But it does seem to me that the memoirs that collect the best reviews and most accolades are the ones where the author has bravely bared his or her soul, threw those long-locked family closets open and aired them out. You don't have to be sordid or cruel about it and you don't have to try to be shocking. Just lay out some truths, that's probably good enough. You might be surprised how freeing it can be.

So, Dear Reader, shovel the coal into the firebox on

your powerful engine and charge on down the track. Chug, chug, chug, stacking those pages. If I can come to grips with, and overcome my childhood physical and emotional challenges, and put them out there for public scrutiny, you can too!

CHAPTER EIGHT

Food For Thought

*"There's no agony like having
an untold story inside you."*

TRUMAN CAPOTE

I want you to be successful in this memoir-writing endeavor. I want to be encouraging, on your team, Pal. Please begin or continue working on your memoir. It could be more important than even you know. You have a story to tell. So, let's keep exploring here.

By the way, let me remind you, it's my opinion that you don't have to sell a million copies of your memoir or sell a million dollars worth to be successful. It'll be nice if you do, but just reach for your own goals, your own numbers, I just want to help get you going. Finish your memoir, not your whole life story, just an interesting slice of it. And when you complete it, and write it as well as you can, bingo! Then you can say you've succeeded!

I've discussed memoirs that have lots of drama and

violence, and those are good emotional aspects to grab the reader and keep him/her going. But now I want to be sure to give humor a serious look too. It seems to me that humorous writers often are given a bit more slack than more serious writers. Consider the "memoirs" of David Sadaris and Patrick McManus, just to pick a couple. While their works often provide raucous laughter, at times when I read their books I'm quite distracted by the outlandish claims obviously crafted for maximum humor. Don't get me wrong, I love to laugh. Some people call these exaggerated works of humor "memoir." I do not. They are obviously pushing the facts so far outside the envelope of truth that they can only be called "tongue-in-cheek" or simply works of humor. In my opinion, while they may be based on real stories, they do not qualify as memoirs.

Having said that, now I want to praise humor. So, so many stories never would have gotten the traction they did without the insertion of humor here and there bringing unexpected smiles, chuckles and knee-slapping responses from the readers. Humor keeps the pages turning and brings relief to ultra-serious situations. A bit of humor can make or break a book, it doesn't have to be full of cleverly crafted jokes, include slap-stick or be outrageously side-splitting. Even a little sly wording while looking back at a situation can add a welcome smile. If there's any tasteful way for you to slip laughter between the pages, do it. If your memoir is very serious, add humor judiciously, but add it. Readers will thank you.

If your story is quite sober there are usually places where a pinch of humor will be just the ticket! Consider a little sleeper of a movie a few years back called "Undertaking Betty." The male star is Alfred Molina, playing a well-established undertaker in a small English village. The new undertaker in town is played by Christopher Walken who is up to all kinds of creative ways to gain more of the undertaking business. It's an hilarious plot, outrageous for sure, but I wanted to point out what can be done even with a deadly-serious situation (undertaking) and a bit of imagination. Admittedly, this is an extreme example, and certainly fiction, but, I believe, still worth mentioning.

My own memoir, "Kid On Fire," has a very serious core of domestic violence, alcoholism, knifings, shootings, etc. but still I try to slip in some lighthearted surprises here and there. It just makes the reading so much more pleasant if you can do it. The writing is more fun too. As promised, I will include my award-winning chapter, "Going To St. John's," later in this book. It's an easier, more fun take on my first day at an orphanage, an otherwise less-than-pleasant experience. It always elicits snickers and laughter when I read it publicly. But, remember, humor can be out of place or distasteful if not used properly. Again I say, trust your gut, read passages aloud to yourself to gauge them. Sometimes humor just doesn't fit well. Always strive to be respectful.

A modern memoir is an interesting animal and is not exclusively made up of only pure extractions from one's memory. If you haven't worked in this genre before, this may be a bit of a surprise to you, but it's true. I've talked about filling in gaps in the story, about transitioning from one time to another and about recreating conversations, but now let's discuss reflecting and musing.

Chug, chug, chug! As you move on down your story track, stacking pages, filling the boxcars, pulling freely from your memory bank, you might want to pause now and again and reflect from your present day age and perspective, muse a bit how an incident affected you, perhaps even changed you. You're a different person today than you were when your past life was taking place.

For instance, you might write something like this from "Kid On Fire:"

Of course, I had no idea at the time when they brought me to the orphanage that I'd never see my mother alive again and how my life was about to change drastically. I was just playing games in my own mind thinking I didn't really have to follow their rules because Mama would be out of the hospital in a week or so, or Dad would sneak back into town to get us, avoiding the cops who were looking for him. When the older boys told us we'd be there forever just like them I'd chuckle inside knowing they were dead wrong. I had no idea how long into my life those times would haunt me. So many years of reliving over and over the tough months and that horrible night that brought us there. Decades later I'd still be looking over my shoulder back to those days and nights that shook me to the core.

As people read your memoir they think not just about the past you're describing to them, and what happened then, but most folks begin to wonder also about the present-day you, the older person writing about their younger self. Obviously you survived the ordeals well enough to put thoughts to paper (or screen). They become a bit curious about the person you are now, as you write.

Take the award-winning memoir by Holocaust survivor, Elie Wiesel. Most readers know before they begin the first page that Wiesel was in a Jewish death camp during World War II. They've heard about the book perhaps or recognize his name. In any event they realize as they read about the unimaginable ghastly times in the camp that Wiesel not only survived but is indeed sane enough, whole and intelligent enough to document the terrible ordeal... to write about his younger self as a boy observing cruelty, starvation, human suffering and death daily. The reader begins to understand how the older author looks at life, begins to appreciate the perspective of a person who has gone through such a nightmare and feels he must tell about it so humanity will never repeat the unspeakable Nazi crimes against humanity.

As Wiesel shows us daily life in the prison camp, he also reflects back as the adult he is now, at the time of the writing, to help give us perspective, help us put the story into context. Doing so will give your own story depth.

"...to remain silent and indifferent is the greatest sin of all.."
"Never shall I forget that night, the first night in camp, which has turned my life into one long night, seven times cursed and seven times sealed." Elie Wiesel

Let's look at a wonderfully told memoir by Sudie Gal titled "DOLLARS TO DONUTS: A Family's Strain of Insanity, My Stormy Walk of Faith Through It, And That Whole Crazy Mother-Daughter Thing." Notice the easy conversational tone...

Being the third child in the family, I was born May 30, 1949, or May 31, 1949, depending upon whose record you would choose to go with—my mother's, or that of the law of the land at the time! Yep. Born at 11:38 pm on May 30, 1949, in Portland, Oregon, at Emanuel Hospital, I was a statistical anomaly confounded by Daylight Savings Time, which was being instituted in patchwork starts and stops around the country during the twenty years following World War II. Hence, my recorded time of birth on my official State of Oregon Birth Certificate was 12:38 am, May 31, 1949. Daylight Savings Time. However! My mother absolutely refused to acknowledge this silly jockeying with the time business! My birthday would not be anything other than May 30th—being the stubborn, contrary rebel that she was. She was 32 when I was born. Periodically throughout her life, she would, in her own words, "take on City Hall," a term she was so fond of, a term I learned from her in living context. This terminology would further apply to anyone else who got in her way. Fire and feistiness. I inherited, absorbed and personified a fair amount of that fight as well in my lifetime.

Wow, this brief passage gives us a clear picture of Sudie Gal's mother, a fire-breather you wouldn't want to cross! In this memoir we're shown what a terrific mother the woman was until dementia began to settle in and then nothing pleased her, her imagination ran wild, she mistrusted everyone and condemned most of them. Eventually her mental disease and temper poisoned the entire family and blew it apart.

The story unravels in realistic descriptions and vivid scenes as we track the battles between the two women who once were so close, and the mother's eventual decline. Any adult who is battling with a senile and/or angry parent, especially in a mother-daughter situation, will find this book especially enlightening. I highly recommend it. I don't wish dementia on any family.

CHAPTER NINE

Going To St. John's

As promised, here's my award-winning
chapter from "Kid On Fire..."

*I was eight the first time we landed in the orphanage. My
brother, Buddy, was ten and our sister, Darlene, the oldest at
eleven. We each carried our few belongings in paper bags and as
the nuns greeted us they had their noses in the bags right away
looking for I'm-not-sure-what.*

*We'd walked past St. John's Orphanage many times that
year since moving from Oregon to North Dakota. It was an
imposing four-story, brick building just off Seventh Avenue in
Fargo and commonly called "The Foundling Home." I didn't
even know what a "foundling" was, but I soon figured it out.*

*The nuns whisked Darlene off to the girls floor and Buddy
and I to the boys.*

*It was 1950 and we'd been living on the edge a couple years. Dad
couldn't find steady work and eventually fell in with the wrong*

people. They had a paint shop in Fargo where they'd paint cars and sell them. A couple agents from the FBI started coming around our hotel room, asking us questions about Dad. It seems there was some uncertainty as to the rightful owners of the cars they were selling.

We'd been living in a rundown hotel on the rough side of town near the Red River waterfront about a year, the five of us sharing one bed: Dad, Mama and Darlene at the head, me and Buddy wedged in between the legs at the foot. A common bathroom down the hall. Since we were originally from milder Oregon, our clothes sorely underestimated the severe North Dakota winters and soon our teachers had a clothing drive just for us Burns kids.

Mama started doing maid work at the hotel and we'd get leftovers from the diner on the street level, so we were eating better than we had for sometime. We had few toys but Buddy and I made up our own war game using beer bottle caps and enjoyed it most of all. The common caps were soldiers, more special ones sergeants and the rarest ones were generals. There was never a shortage of beer bottle caps and our collection grew into the hundreds. Miller High Life Beer and Schlitz were pretty common, and we had quite a few 7 Up bottle caps as well, Mama used it for mixer with whiskey or wine. We would meticulously line up our armies in even rows on the wooden floor and play for hours.

Our parents were drinking pretty heavily and often fighting, so Darlene would come up with distractions to get us kids out of the room when we weren't in school. Sometimes we'd go walking, go to movie matinees, admission 12 cents each, or if it was Sunday she'd take us down the street to a basement Sunday service. The message was delivered by a Salvation Army Officer to a small audience of mostly old wino men in various states of sobriety. There I learned a little about Heaven, which sounded pretty nice, and Hell, which I didn't want anything to do with. So I did my best to behave when I could.

46

But before long Dad was run off by the FBI agents, Mama went to the hospital for drug treatment, and there we were packing up to go to the foundling home. Darlene didn't think it would be a good idea to take our bottle caps, but I wasn't about to leave my rare generals. I stuffed them into a front pocket. Then I thought, "What good are generals without armies?" So when Darlene wasn't looking I stuffed my sergeants in my other front pocket. Then as many soldiers as I could into my back pockets and we left.

One of the nuns, Sister Agnes, had some long dark hairs on her chin and she was impatient. She brought us each a small pile of folded clothes.

"You boys strip off your dirty things and throw them into this bucket," she said. "Then take a quick bath, get dressed and come downstairs to eat. We can't wait dinner on you!" And she left. I'd never seen nuns up close before and I couldn't help being a little afraid of them. And I wondered why they dressed so much like witches, but with different headgear.

"Hurry up!" Buddy told me as he finished dressing after his bath. Then he hurried off downstairs.

I dried off quickly and pulled on the white undershorts from the pile. They were stiff and very tight with large buttons at the waist and fly. I was struggling with the waist button when Sister Agnes reappeared.

"What are you doing? You've got to hurry!"

"I can't get this buttoned. It's too tight."

"It's got to be tight to stay up on your skinny behind." She grabbed the waistband. "Suck in your belly." She pulled the shorts snug around my middle and worked the button through the buttonhole. Then with a little difficulty and a grunt, she managed to get the fly buttoned as well. "Now finish dressing. We're not holding dinner for you!" And she left in a huff.

The clothes they'd given me included practically new socks, without a single hole, a pullover shirt with little brown and yellow stripes going across, clean-but-ugly rusty-orange-colored bib overalls. I hated them from the git. But I also knew if I wanted any dinner I'd have to wear them. I dressed and dropped my old underclothes and shirt into the bucket. It took me a few minutes to figure out what to do with all the bottle caps in my pants pockets. I did the best thing I could figure out and when the old pants were empty I dropped them into the bucket too and hurried downstairs.

Sister Agnes met me at the bottom. "You almost missed dinner. Go git in line!" And as I tried to rush past her she swatted me on the behind with her wooden ruler. But it didn't hurt because she hit a pocketful of caps. Chink! *"What's that? What've you got in there?" She grabbed me by the shoulder to stop me.*

"It's... they're ...caps."

"Caps! What kind of caps?"

"They're my bottle caps, and I'm keeping them!"

She smacked me on the other side of my rump with the ruler. Chink!

"For Heaven's sake, are they in that pocket too?" She spun me around, noticed every pocket bulging, tapped each with the ruler. Chink! Chink! Chink! *"Just how many bottle caps do you have in there?"*

"Maybe, uh, about one-hundred-seventy-six. Just my best ones."

She began flipping caps out of my pockets onto the wooden floor. "You smell like a brewery!"

I liked the smell, it reminded me of my dad.

Sister Agnes emptied every pocket onto the wooden floor, even the generals hidden in the front bib pocket. I was desperate and started yelling.

"You're not throwing them away! They're my army!" I tried to pick them up but she held me tight by the back of the shirt collar.

The ruckus brought several kids and the other nun out of the cafeteria to see what was going on between one of the new boys and Sister Agnes. Some of the kids were snickering but the cafeteria nun was calm, almost smiling.

"Sister Agnes, put them in a paper bag, we'll keep them for him in storage. Now, David, come and eat." I found out that her name was Sister Mary and I just loved her right away. And she already knew my name!

Later, at bedtime, I was having a devil of a time trying to unbutton the fly in my undershorts. The button was too big and I just couldn't get it through the buttonhole. And I had to pee so bad! I was working at it, hopping on one foot, then the other when Sister Agnes showed up for the evening bunk count.

"What is wrong now, boy?"

"I can't …get this button undone. It's stuck and I really gotta pee!"

"Just pull them down."

"I tried. They're too tight!"

"Hold still. Let me see that button. She struggled with the fly button as I jiggled and hopped up and down. "Hold still!" She began mumbling under her breath. "Who sewed these huge buttons..."

All of a sudden I couldn't hold back the pee anymore and it came rushing out!

"Oh, stop! Stop it!" Sister Agnes jerked her hands back and flipped pee off her fingers.

"I can't," I said. Oh Lord, I thought, I'm going to Hell for sure. I just peed on a nun and I'm not even Catholic.

And that was my first day at St. John's Orphanage.

Let's go behind the scenes a bit with this original piece and pick at it a little and see how it developed and what makes it tick. First off, let's look at the general mood of my chapter. It's pretty lighthearted. The incident came from my own life at a tough time for my family but we kids were told by adults in our lives that the orphanage stay would be very brief and we'd be back with our mother after her short stay in the hospital. I think that's what allowed me to write an amusing piece. If it had taken place right after my mother's death, such a piece would be in poor taste.

I wanted to keep it light because it pretty much happened that way and it preceded some pretty serious topics coming up in my memoir. I wanted to show how we were living at the time, but at the same time I know too much heaviness can really bring down the reader and I look for moments of amusement and entertainment to bring some balance. I could have written this particular scene either way but I took the lighter approach when I saw the opportunity.

Just for your information, I wrote it the way I wanted and slanted it toward the funny bone. The scene was pretty true to fact but I reshaped it a little for better story-telling. The hotel scenes are right on; Dad and the hot cars and the FBI, both parents heavy into alcohol, Mom taking psychedelic drugs and sent to dry out, five of us to one bed, Dad escaping out of state. Buddy and I had amazing bottle cap collections. I got in trouble with the first nun, honestly it was mostly over wearing those awful orange bib overalls, but I used the caps for a bit more amusement. In the end it was told pretty much the way it happened, or very darn close.

It's acceptable to reshape an incident a bit using artistic license. Just don't overdue it or you'll wander into a work of fiction. But again, memoir is not journalism.

CHAPTER TEN

Chugging Along

*"Living a conscious and reflective life is a prerequisite
for writing a memoir of substance."*

JUDITH BARRINGTON

By now you're chugging along at a good clip, maybe even breakneck speed, stacking pages, filling those boxcars! Or you soon will be! You've defined the perimeters of this particular slice-of-life memoir. You've opened a fresh file for notes and ideas, bits of description or snatches of conversation. You've decided where to start, played a bit with your on-the-page voice. You're watching closely to keep it consistent. And, by golly, the pages are really starting to stack up. You're on your way, actually writing a memoir. Feels good, doesn't it!?

Don't rush it too much, pause to give thought to a structured scene. Rework it later perhaps. Think about where you were at a specific time. Put your story into context. Perhaps you're familiar with the term "talking heads." Talking heads occur in a piece of writing where two or more people are having a conversation with no context. This person speaks, then that one. We're not shown any setting, are they in a field or downtown New York City's Fifth Avenue? We can't see their faces or clothing. Are they in denim, in 17th Century Europe's finest fashion or grass skirts? Our people, our scenes must be shown in context!

For instance: *It was late Spring 1973, Fred, dressed only in yellow undershorts, was face down on the bathroom floor of his old Airstream trailer in the overgrown trailer park at the edge of Buffalo, New York. Dawn shot shafts of bright sunlight through the small window reflecting off the bloody pool of water on the fake tile flooring.*

And so on. Give us context. Make it fun. Give it some context so the reader knows where we are and what he/she should be visualizing. Get them right into the story with a bit of detail.

Another example:
I knew I'd be in trouble when I went inside our house because there was blood spots on my white t-shirt. I was six that year, as I remember it, and everyone was hovered around the TV talking about a man from Earth walking on the moon. I had crashed my tricycle right beside the big cactus next to our driveway and knocked out my loose tooth. Daddy, Mamma and Aunt Ruth were all smoking cigarettes and at first I couldn't tell if the guy on the moon was kicking up dust or if was smoke in our house. The Phoenix dust blew in behind me as I left the door wide open.

"Hey look!" I said, through my tears, holding up my tooth. "Can I put this under my pillow tonight?"

Daddy blew out a big cloud of smoke, didn't even turn my way. "Shhh! Close the door. There's a man on the moon!"

You can tell from this example that it's probably a dry summer day in Phoenix, Arizona and you know from the TV excitement that it's 1969 when Neil Armstrong was on the moon. It's good to work in a historic fact giving your story a time and place instantly without always having to just write the date. We have the boy's age, his white t-shirt and tricycle to gauge things by. We have a desert home in the late sixties, the adults smoking cigarettes and glued to the TV set. That's enough information for us to begin imagining the scene in our minds. Houston, we have context!

Chug, chug, chug! Keep stacking those pages! Keep checking for lively verbs, opportunities for good scenes and bits of description. Write up close now and then, create scenes, and then at more of a distance as you bring us through time. You might decide to pause the passage of time, slow it down, and a while later it might seem natural to stretch it out. That's fine, telescope time for your convenience of storytelling. But, please, be sure to let the readers know where we are; don't make them guess if we're back in the flashback, present time or what? *Let's see, how old would the author be now?* Don't make them guess.

Don't try to get even with that ornery cousin in your memoir. If he did something awful, and you want to include it, go ahead, but just state it factually. Don't try to look all Goody-Two-Shoes and him all devilish. We all have some good and bad. And, remember, this is your memoir and you don't have to write about everything bad you ever did. But try to be fair.

Sometimes you might want to insert yourself, as you are today, and look back at your past, hopefully with a more mature eye. Share some grown-up wisdom with your audience.

Of course at the time I didn't really know why FBI detectives came to our room when Dad was gone, asking questions. Mama said they needed to find Norris because his shop was empty and he was gone. She said Dad wasn't in trouble. And, being the youngest, nobody told me much more. But looking back over the years, now I've figured out he and Norris must've been stealing cars, painting them new colors and selling them.

I could be wrong, but whatever it was the FBI wanted with Dad, he didn't stick around long enough for them to find him. It took me years to figure out that Mama wasn't just drinking heavily after Dad left but she was taking drugs too. I had no idea what that meant at the tender age of eight.

This example I plucked out of my memoir, "Kid On Fire," and for the record, I'd already fixed it in time and place for the reader. You can see how my adult brain tried to fill in the sparse story I'd been told when I was eight. Sometimes that's about all you can do. But do look back from your older perspective once in a while.

Okay, we've walked down this writerly path together, hopped on the memoir train, stoked the fire box, chugged down the tracks and stacked pages. We've had a few reminders and we've tried to weave our theme through our story. We've Begun. We've Middled, and now our tome is arcing toward the End. The caboose is in sight rounding the bend. Slow down the train, bring things together, wrap it up.

We stop the train where the footpath crosses, in this case at Chapter Ten. The Memoir Train slows, blows off its clouds of steam and screeches to a stop. We hop off, gather our stacks of pages from every box car and carry the tall pile down the foot path toward the publishing depot!

CHAPTER ELEVEN

Publishing

*"I was working on the proof of one of my
poems all the morning, and took out a comma.
In the afternoon I put it back in again."*

OSCAR WILDE

The publishing world has changed immeasurably over the last couple decades. The old way of sending a letter of inquiry to a literary agency via the post office, or even email and then sitting back and waiting for weeks or months for a request for the complete manuscript, are just that, the old way. And if you were lucky, using that old method, and an agent actually agreed to take on your project, then you could work on rewrites for weeks or months with an editor. Then wait while the agent tried to get a publisher interested. Maybe more back and forth, more editing, then deal negotiations. The best an author could really hope for was a deal with an established publisher that would agree to put the book out, stand behind it and help sell copies. And give the author a good royalty for his/her work.

The author could often wind up with very little advertising or backup work, a small royalty, maybe 10% of the cover price, and it could take a year or more to get the book out to the public. There were some exceptions to this scenario every year, some quicker and more lucrative deals for the authors, perhaps for an extremely hot property or a celebrity writer. But the more common road to publishing included years of searches to find an agent and perhaps as long or longer to have one's work accepted by a decent publisher. Sad but true.

And believe me, there are scammers out there waiting for you to contact them about publishing your work. I have been a victim of an unsavory agent myself. Several years ago I had some children's stories I was shopping around and sent them to an agent in Texas. Lots of back and forth emails later, I agreed to cover postage for the agent to send out the collection to prospective publishers. Even over time, it wasn't very much money but if she had a list of clients it may have added up for her. My questions to her increased and finally I received several pages of excuses over several weeks including that her partner and husband had come down with a serious illness and she couldn't travel to publisher's offices like she used to.

To make a long story short, months later I received a letter from a Texas sheriff informing me that my stories were being held in evidence while the literary agency was being investigated for fraud. It came to light that apparently the "agent" agreed to represent authors' works, but did not actually attempt to sell anything. She just tried to scam her clients out of whatever money she could. Fortunately, she only got a small amount of money "to cover postage" from me. The bad part was the damage it was doing to young authors and their confidence.

Please be careful who you trust. Do some background checking. The Association of Author's Representatives is a good place to begin.

With the explosion of the Internet world and proliferation of on-line publishers, e-readers, as well as the amazing growth of electronic retailer Amazon, and others, the publishing industry has changed dramatically in the past several years. And it is still changing.

These days new authors have avenues open to them that weren't even dreamed of when I used to submit my early efforts to publishers and agents. Nowadays authors don't have to drop their manuscript off at the post office and wait weeks or months for acceptance, rejection or any acknowledgment at all.

I was slow to come around to the thought of self-publishing or electronic publishing for e-readers. As far as self-publishing, many of our favorite writers of long ago published their own works. People like Virginia Woolf, Ben Franklin and Edgar Allen Poe, to name just a few. It didn't seem to hurt their reputations in spite of some publishing snobs of today who hold firmly to the belief that "traditional" publishing is the only respected path to consider.

In my opinion, the big publishing houses have been slow to come around to the new, revolutionary methods available these days. For the most part they're stuck in the last century, as are the royalties they offer authors. It takes a good agent working for you to even get your manuscript in front of a publisher for consideration. If you're lucky enough to land an honest agent he'll take 15% of your money if he finds a publisher interested in taking on the product of your blood, sweat and buckets of tears. Then, perhaps, the publisher will assign an editor to work with you doing rewrites to turn your book more toward their liking, as well as catching errors, of course. Back and forth it goes until you reach some kind of compromise, then off to the printer.

You may get some say in the cover design and a little input with the cash-strapped sales department. Eventually, in a year or eighteen months your traditionally-published book will come out. You may have received a nominal advance-against-future-royalties, and may be expected to pay some of your book tour expenses out of pocket, if you get a tour at all. And the publisher will likely issue you royalty checks for about 10% of the cover price for your creation. That cover price will be determined by the publisher.

One of the things new authors struggle with is platform. And your platform is merely your presence or following. For instance, a newspaper columnist has a built-in readership of perhaps hundreds of people or thousands. That's his or her platform and it can be used to help sell his new book. A friend of mine, M. Pax, writes science fiction novels and has built up quite an on-line following using Facebook, Twitter and the like, rather successfully. That's her platform. When publishers are deciding whether to buy a manuscript, one of the aspects they strongly consider is the author's platform. Does this author already have a following or not...what is the platform?

I suppose there might be a little more prestige in going the traditional route, with a well-known publisher, then again, maybe not so much anymore. You certainly have more control and higher royalty percentages if you self-publish or e-publish and your book could be out and for sale in days or weeks at the most. Amazon e-publishers pay between 50% and 70% of the retail price to you in royalties! I must note here though, the electronic version of your book, to be read on-line or with electronic readers, must be sold at much lower cover prices to compete. While Amazon's Kindle publishes the electronic version, its partner Create Space publishes a paperback version of your work, and if you're careful how you sign up with Amazon you are welcome to sell your book through the several other e-publishers as well.

Recommended pricing for e-books are low because it is so much cheaper for the publisher to bring it out in electronic format than compared to paper copies which must be printed, bound, stored and shipped. E-books sell for $3.99 perhaps, but look at the immediate millions of on-line prospects that might buy them with a quick click on the computer! The Amazon paperbacks retail for $14.99 to $9.99 to be competitive, but for both formats you actually get to name the retail price yourself, unheard of in the traditional world. They also offer audio book sales which can add up to a pretty penny as well.

Let's round off the figures and look at a little math here.

If you sell one book for $18.00 with a traditional publisher your take is about 10% or about $1.80 for each copy sold coming to you. That's about $1,800 per 1000 and $18,000 per ten thousand. If your book is really starting to catch fire and you sell 100,000 copies, your take is $180,000. Now we're talking serious money. Add paperback sales later, perhaps another $10.00 at 10% is 1.00 or $10,000 per 100,000 sales. $180,000 + $100,000 = $280,000 for your share. Not too bad.

Now let's look at an Amazon example. E-book price $4.00, and your take at 70% (or so, percentages may change) is about $2.80 per book. Per 100,000 e-books it equals $280,000. Plus the paperback coming out at the same time add $10.00 x 100,000 at a 50% royalty (depending) = another $500,000. Together that's $780,000 for your personal account! Estimate another several thousand for audio book sales and we're knocking at the Million Dollar Memoir door! If your selling is going well the first couple years, then you may hit the big M$M the third year of sales! And trust me, given the choice, a book shopper will probably hit the "buy" button and shell out $3.99 a heck of a lot quicker than $18.00 for the traditional hardback book. I expect you'll sell lots more copies on-line in today's market.

And if things are going well for your book, traditional publishers will notice and may make you a sweet offer as well.

Once your book is completed and published, take a breath and celebrate a little. Then, I advise you to start your next book. You're a writer now, write. Just think, after that second book is finished and published, you'll have two money streams of royalties flowing into your account.

But for right now, as you complete your first memoir, I am so proud of you! Thank you for perhaps letting me help you along the way a bit. Congratulations, author!

Amazon has programs to help put your book on certain lists to get it out there in front of more eyes, more prospects. One of the criteria for doing this is that you get some early reviews of your book. Let me ask a favor of you; if you found this book helpful, or some of the tips and encouragement to your liking, please take a moment and write a short review to Amazon for me. Stay in touch and later I can do the same for you. Thank you so much for your time. Write on!

Resource List

Kid On Fire by David H Burns, (memoir, coming 2016).

DOLLARS TO DONUTS: A Family's Strain of Insanity, My Stormy Walk of Faith Through It, And That Whole Crazy Mother-Daughter Thing by Sudie Gal, (memoir, coming 2016).

Day Follow Night by David (DH) Burns, (2005, a somewhat biographical novel).

Angela's Ashes by Frank McCourt, (1996 memoir).

Writing the Memoir, From Truth to Art by Judith Barrington, (1997 memoir instruction).

Lifesaving by Judith Barrington, (2000 memoir).

The Glass Castle by Janette Walls, (2005 memoir).

The Liar's Club by Mary Karr, (1995 memoir).

Writing Life Stories by Bill Roorbach, (1998 memoir instruction).

October Sky by Homer H Hickam, Jr., (1998 memoir, originally published as *Rocket Boys).*

Bird By Bird, by Anne Lamott (1994 writing instruction)`

An American Childhood by Annie Dillard, (1987 memoir).

A Child Called It, One Child's Courage to Survive by Dave Pelzer, (1995 memoir).

This Boy's Life by Tobias Wolff, (1989 memoir).

Fearless Confessions, A Writer's Guide to Memoir by Sue William Silverman, (2009 memoir instruction).

Writing and Selling Your Memoir by Paula Balzer, (2011 memoir instruction).

Brain On Fire by Susannah Cahalan, (2012 memoir).

Night by Elie Wiesel, (2006 memoir).

The Wink of the Zenith, The Shaping of a Writer's Life by Floyd Skloot (2008 memoir).

The Self-Publishing School, webinars and excerpts by Chandler Bolt

The Publishing Authority, Workshops with Linda Stirling

Online Writing Coach, Debbie Drum

Online Writing Coach, Amy Harrop

About the Author

DAVID H. BURNS has been writing since he was age five and he discovered that Superman's day job was newspaper reporting as Clark Kent. David has written dozens of short stories, one novel, *Day Follow Night: From Chaos To Redemption,* magazine articles, children's stories and has written for five different newspapers including the *Oregon Journal,* now defunct, and *The Oregonian* both of Portland.

Losing his parents early, David grew up in many different living situations including the back of a flatbed truck, in shacks, with various family friends, an assortment of relatives, an orphanage and three foster homes. As near as he can recollect he attended thirteen schools in twelve years and lived in at least 43 places during his lifetime.

His young years were emotionally marked with alcoholic parents and foster parents as well as extreme domestic violence. At times his family was without food or heat in the cruel Washington, Oregon, Minnesota and North Dakota winters.

Later he served as a Sonar Technician for fours years plus in the Navy on a Destroyer where he sailed through angry ocean storms, witnessed rough and tumble waterfronts in over 30 far-flung locations half-way 'round the globe and survived a spectacular collision at sea. He was involved in three serious car wrecks, two knifings, two shootings and countless fights, but somehow The Good Lord saw fit to eventually bring the right people into his life and save him for better times.

After hospitalization for a nervous breakdown David had a number of counseling sessions which were very helpful in sorting out an alcoholic, violent and chaotic past. His passion now is to help others.

David began seriously studying modern memoirs several years ago and considers himself *The Memoir Junkie*. He now lives and writes in the peaceful outback of rural Oregon with his wife Susie of over 47 years in a lovely hillside home with stunning views.

What he hopes will be his own Million Dollar Memoir, *Kid On Fire,* is set to be released in 2016.

Notes

_____

_____

_____

_____

_____

_____

_____

_____

_____

_____

_____

_____

_____

_____

_____

_____

_____

_____

_____

_____

_____

Notes

Notes

Made in the USA
Lexington, KY
18 February 2018